Water Sampling

Water Sampling

a library of loops for your life

by
Stan Dotson

dedicated to Kim,
who teaches me how to find the flow
and be in my element

Table of Contents

an introduction to Water Sampling

Not too long ago, whenever I heard the word *sample*, I thought about food (the sampler platter at a local restaurant), or surveys (the random sample) . But thanks to hip hop, the word now has a musical meaning. Sampling in the recording industry happens when an artist takes a piece of someone else's song and weaves it into their own song. When that small piece of sampled music gets inserted into a new song and is played repeatedly throughout the song it is called a "loop." Some artists have sued others over this practice, saying that it's stealing, but the Supreme Court has ruled that it isn't, explaining that all music borrows from other music and there's no such thing as a completely "original" piece of work.

Our lives are a lot like that. We are the product of a lot of "loops" that get inserted into our daily experience. This reflection booklet asks you to do some sampling of your own. Each week there will be a sacred story from scripture, a short "loop" from that story, and a random sample from my own life story. Try "sampling" these loops and stories - see where they connect with your life experience, and how they could add to the "soundtrack" of your own life.

There are three sections to the reflection book, building a **knowledge** base of self-discovery, a **skill** set of active listening, and a **values** commitment of courage. Taken together, all of these are designed to get your own creative juices flowing, to give you some imagery that will get you deeper into the flow of your own life.

Part One

Navigating the River of Self-Discovery

River of Self-Discovery

Week One: *Influence*
who made you that way?

Sampling the Sacred Story

Jesus then appeared, arriving at the Jordan River from Galilee. He wanted John to baptize him. John objected, "I'm the one who needs to be baptized, not you!" But Jesus insisted. "Do it. God's work, putting things right all these centuries, is coming together right now in this baptism."
–Matthew 3:13-15

The Loop

God's work . . . is coming together right now.

What if God has been working throughout the centuries
to make you who you are?

Two Rooms
a random sampling of *influences*

Bilbo used to say there was only one Road;
that it was like a great river:
its springs were at every doorstep,
and every path was its tributary.
—*J.R.R. Tolkien, Fellowship of the Ring*

I went to my first rock concert when I was twelve years old. I saw the group *Styx*; they were on their *Grand Illusion* tour. It was the same year that I first saw the contemporary Christian group *Truth*. I didn't know then that "Styx" was the name of a river in Greek mythology, associated with truth-telling. If I had known, I may not have had sense enough to appreciate the connection between *Styx* and *Truth*. Anyway, from my musical tastes at the time, you can safely conclude that I was trying to figure out who I was.

This much I knew: I was the son of Dal and Edith Dotson, earthy people who loved each other and enjoyed music and read lots of books and tended their garden with great care and had a deep faith and a lively sense of humor. I was the grandson of mill workers and farmers. I was the brother of a long-haired hippie and a clean-cut Vietnam soldier. Because my grandmother lived with us, and because she had eleven other children besides my Dad, there was a steady stream of aunts and uncles and cousins coming to visit. The men sat in the living room and smoked cigarettes and told stories, and the women sat in the kitchen and nibbled on leftovers and told stories. I was drawn to both rooms — to the stories that came out of both rooms. The men talked about the war and the Sunday School lesson. The women talked about family. The conversation in both rooms flowed out of the same river, a river of shared history that bound all sorts of unlikely people together — hippies and warriors, Democrats and Republicans, bootleggers and Baptist deacons.

All these "tributaries" helped me figure out who I am and what I stand for. While the stream of my life has passed through many experiences, and is deeper, with a stronger current, in some ways, I'm still doing what I was doing as a twelve year old — I am trying to figure out who I am. My musical tastes have changed – these days I listen to the Beatles and sing old Baptist hymns. But I like to think I'm still on a quest for *Truth*, and there are times when it feels like all that my work is part of some *Grand Illusion*. When those times come, I try and remember the stories of the living room and kitchen, and I simply pray that whatever I do with my life will somehow be a fitting *tribute* to my *tributaries*.

Sampling the Influences of Your Life. . .

What does the sacred story and these random
thoughts on *influences* bring to your mind?
Who are the most influential people in your life?
How has God worked through them to make you
who you are? Sample your own life experience and
draw, doodle, or write whatever comes to mind.

River of Self-Discovery

Week Two: *Change*
how have you been transformed?

Sampling the Sacred Story

John said, "I'm baptizing you here in the river.
The main character in this drama, to whom I'm
a mere stagehand, will ignite the kingdom life,
a fire, the Holy Spirit within you,
changing you from the inside out."
−Luke 3:16

The Loop

changing you from the inside out.

What if God is igniting a fire right now,
that will change us from the inside out?

Tadpole
random sampling of *changes*

Be the change you want to see in the world.
–Mahatma Gandhi

It was a blast from the past; I had not heard his voice in well over twenty-five years. It was Tad, my cousin, calling me to get advice on a potential college for his teenage daughter. It's hard to explain how much of a shock this was. Tad, short for Tadpole, was the nickname he got when he was a young boy exploring streams and creeks, fascinated by all the life he found there. Tad's mother, my aunt Moleta, died from cancer when he was nine or ten, and life for him and his family pretty much fell apart after her death. Uncle Ed, Tad's father, dealt with the death through heavier and heavier drinking, until alcoholism took control of his life. Tad came to live with us when he was around 12, and it was my first exposure to anyone with severe emotional disturbance. He was kicked out of one school after another, fell into the "wrong crowd," began experimenting with drugs, and it wasn't long before the experimentation evolved into a way of life. Somewhere along the way, during those teenage years, we lost touch with Tad.

Without going into twenty-five years worth of transformation, the short story is that Tad found himself as a homeless, addicted young adult, and turned out to be one of the "lucky" or "blessed" ones, depending on your world view. Twenty-five years later, he emerged from a mighty river of change; he was a family man, with a wife and two teenage children, a good job, a good home in a good neighborhood.

Sometime after his phone call, Tad brought his family to town for a visit. I looked at this kind, funny, smart man, and thought about that extremely troubled teen. It reminded me of the resilience of young people. No matter how torn up and chaotic life gets, given the right kinds of circumstances and relationships, there is a chance for survival. There are many whose stories do not turn out so well, but Tad's story gives me hope every time I hear about a young person who drops out of a meaningful life.

Looking back on that year Tad lived with us, I realize that he was not the only one going through change. The experience changed me, in ways I was not aware of at the time. It opened up the sheltered world I had inhabited.

He doesn't go by Tad or Tadpole anymore; he is Tim. But I can't imagine a more appropriate nickname for a young boy who swam in the river of change, for a child who started out in a suffocating environment and developed the capacity to breathe hope and take leaps of faith.

Sampling the Changes of Your Life. . .

What does the sacred story and these random
thoughts on *changes* bring to your mind?
How have you changed over the past year?
What major changes are looming on the horizon for
you right now? How is God involved in those
changes? Sample your own life experience and
draw, doodle, or write what comes to mind.

River of Self-Discovery

Week Three: *Anger*
what makes you mad?

Sampling the Sacred Story

When crowds of people came out for baptism because it was
the popular thing to do, John exploded: "Brood of snakes!
What do you think you're doing slithering down to the river?
Do you think a little water on your snakeskins
is going to deflect God's judgment?
It's your life that must change, not your skin."
–Luke 3:7

The Loop

John exploded.

What if God wants us to get angry sometimes?
What kind of explosive energy is God stirring up in you?

Melting Stony Hearts
random sampling of *anger*

Launch into the deep.
—Jacques Ellul

When I lived in Louisville one of my jobs was helping poor people find resources to pay their light bills each month. It was a real problem for people on fixed incomes, whose power bill ate up most of their monthly check, particularly in the winter months, leaving them with no money left over for medicine or food. Some of the people got tired of begging for charity assistance every month, and they organized a group called POWER — People Outraged With Energy Rates. They channeled their anger into work toward the goal of preventing poor folks from freezing in the winter, by capping the LG&E (Louisville, Gas, and Electric) bills at 10% of monthly incomes.

One of the key neighborhood leaders was an elderly African American woman named Frances Richardson. Frances was the first black person to live in the Clifton neighborhood. When she first moved in and some neighbors painted graffiti on the side of her house, "Nigger Go Home" she simply questioned what they meant, since she was sitting in her home. Her steadfast pursuit of racial justice paid off, and in a few short years she was not only accepted, she was respected as a valuable member of the community, and her neighbors elected her president of the first neighborhood watch association.

Frances became one of the key voices in the POWER movement. She opened up her home every Friday afternoon for POWER meetings. She began every meeting with a reading from the Psalms, generally one of those where the Psalmist cries out to God to hear the prayers of the poor and deal with the evil-doing powerful folks, and then she would pray. These prayers were the only times I ever heard Frances raise her voice. The rest of the time her rage was safely masked by a soft voice and kind smile. But her prayers, which started almost in a whisper, would gradually increase in intensity until they reached the peak of a shouting appeal for God to *melt the stony hearts of those people down at LG&E.*

A couple of years after I left Louisville, someone sent me a newspaper article. LG&E had agreed to a new policy — a Percentage of Income Plan. It seemed stony hearts could be melted after all. Frances taught me that rage and prayer and an organized community could melt away rocks of unfairness so that justice could roll down like waters and righteousness an ever flowing stream.

Sampling the Anger in Your Life. . .

**What does the sacred story and these random
thoughts on *anger* bring to your mind?
What kinds of things irritate you on a daily basis?
What gets you really mad?
How do you think God could use your anger?
Sample your own life experience and draw, doodle,
or write what comes to mind.**

River of Self-Discovery

Week Four: *Grief*
what have you lost?

Sampling the Sacred Story

*Don't you know that all of us who were baptized into
Christ Jesus were baptized into his death?
We were therefore buried with him through baptism into
death in order that, just as Christ was raised from the dead
through the glory of the Father,
we too may live a new life.*
–Romans 6:3-4

The Loop

all of us . . . were baptized into his death

What if there are things in our lives that need to die out
when we are immersed in Christ's death?

Washing Out The Road
random sampling of *grief*

You can fall like the rain, and I will be your river,
winding forever strong and true.
—Kate Campbell

If you live long enough, you're going to lose something you care deeply about. When my wife, Kim, and I were in a class to become foster parents, we learned a lot about the tragic losses at-risk children have to endure. One of the goals of the class was for us to become "loss experts" so that we could help wounded children learn how to grieve, how to deal with all sorts of losses—loss of innocence, loss of parents, loss of trust. As I was in the class, I couldn't help thinking about my dad — I always called him "Pop" — and what he taught me about dealing with loss.

Pop was born and grew up out on a mountain farm called the "Old Place," where Kim and I now live. To get to the Old Place, you have to get off the paved road and drive a mile up a narrow gravel road, steep in places. Heavy rains can be hard on a mountain road. Pop was always careful to keep the drain ditch beside the road clear of leaves and keep the culverts open, so that the water flowing off the mountain would not take the road with it.

Our work together on the Old Place came to an abrupt halt when Pop was diagnosed with cancer. No one in the family was prepared for the floodgate of fear that opened up in us when we heard the doctor say he only had three months to live. Pop had always been our bedrock, and I don't think any of us had ever imagined that he might leave us one day.

One afternoon, a few weeks before he died, Pop talked his doctors into letting him leave the hospital for a short trip. He wanted to go back out to the Old Place. I drove him, and during the 30-minute drive we didn't say much. When I turned onto our gravel road, it suddenly occurred to me that this would be the last time Pop would ever ride up this mountain path, the last time he would see the beautiful Laurel flowers lining the road. I slowed the truck down so we could take it all in, and as the tears streamed down my face, Pop said in a broken voice, "I've spent my whole life trying to teach you boys how to live. Now I've got to try and teach you how to die."

Kim and I now work on the Old Place road, keeping the ditches and culverts clear, and we remember Pop. Even now, there are times when the loss brings on a flood of grief, and sometimes these emotions threaten to wash out my "road"—my path. Heavy loss can be hard on the soul, and I have to make sure and take the time to tend to my own personal drainage ditches and keep my culverts open, so there's always a place for the sadness to flow.

Sampling the Grief of Your Life. . .

What does the sacred story and these random
thoughts on *grief* bring to your mind?
What kinds of things have you lost in your life?
How do you experience grief?
How do you experience God in the midst of sadness?
Sample your own life experience and draw, doodle,
or write what comes to mind.

Part Two

Catching the Waves of
Active Listening

Catching the Waves of Active Listening

Week Five: *Anticipation*
what do you hope to hear?

Sampling the Sacred Story

As soon as Jesus was baptized, he went up out of the water.
At that moment heaven was opened, and he saw the Spirit of
God descending like a dove and alighting on him.
And a voice from heaven said, "This is my Son, whom I love;
with him I am well pleased."

–Matthew 3: 16-17

The Loop

A voice from heaven said. . .

What do you think that voice of God sounded like?
Do you think Jesus expected that message?
What kinds of voices and messages
do you expect to get on a daily basis?
Do you expect God to speak to you through other people?

Listening to the Waves
random sampling of *anticipation*

maggie and milly and molly and may
went down to the beach (to play one day)
and maggie discovered a shell that sang
so sweetly she couldn't remember her troubles. . . .
—ee cummings

I came along fairly late in my parents' life, a surprise baby with two brothers, ten and fifteen years older. By the time I arrived on the scene my folks were pretty much vacationed out and all I could do was look longingly at photo albums with pictures of all the beach trips they took with my two older brothers, Jerry and David. These two still went on beach excursions with their friends, but I was too young to accompany them. David brought me back a seashell when I was six or seven, and he told me I could hear the ocean if I put it up to my ear. I treasured that sea shell and must have listened to it a thousand times before I finally got to go to Garden City Beach with our church youth group and hear up close what the shell had been singing to me all those years.

My dad was fascinated by the concept of sound waves; maybe it was because his job involved repairing musical instruments. Pop had this idea — I don't know where he got it — that sound waves were as constant as ocean waves, that they ebb and flow but never completely die out. He believed that every sound ever made is still traveling by wave through some dimension of space, pulled to and fro by some unseen force of gravity. He was convinced that someone would eventually develop technology to capture those waves, so that we could hear the sounds again—Lincoln giving the Gettysburg address, Jesus preaching his sermon on the mount, the very first bird whistle. Pop anticipated with great expectancy the day when this technology would be available.

It wasn't just the anticipation of capturing sound waves from the past that fascinated him. He carried this same attitude of expectancy with him into everyday experiences, and this made him a great listener. He anticipated ordinary encounters with that same expectancy that he might just hear something significant. I don't remember him ever being bored.

I have come to believe that anticipation is the first and most important tool of listening. I hear the wonders of the ocean from a shell because I expect to. And the reverse is true; if I enter an experience expecting to be bored, I will be. Meanwhile, the waves go on and on, traveling through their dimension of space, waiting for the day when they will be heard once again.

Sampling Your Life. . .

**What does the sacred story and
these random thoughts on *anticipation* bring to
your mind? What do you expect to hear today?
Sample your own life experience
and draw, doodle, or write what comes to mind.**

Catching the Waves of Active Listening

Week Six: *Attention*
What are you stretching toward?

Sampling the Sacred Story

*If you listen carefully to the LORD your God and do what is
right in his eyes, if you pay attention to his commands and
keep all his decrees, I will not bring on you any of the diseases
I brought on the Egyptians, for I am the LORD, who heals you.*
–Exodus 15:26

The Loop

If you listen carefully. . . if you pay attention. . .

What would "listening carefully" to God look like to you?
What are some concrete ways you could demonstrate
that you are paying attention to God?

Attendere
random sampling of *attention*

It's just like the ocean, under the moon.
—Carlos Santana and Rob Thomas

My eighth-grade English teacher, Mr. Martin, was an ex-boxer and military man. Mr. Martin barked orders for us to turn in book reports or recite lines of poetry as if he were our drill sergeant calling us to drop and give him twenty. His favorite part of the English course was word origins. He was an intimidating teacher who scared us into learning the Latin roots of everyday words.

Mr. Martin would give animated lectures on the finer points of English grammar, mixing in stories and demonstrations of his days in the boxing ring. After launching an uppercut and right jab at his shadow opponent, he would shout out with enthusiasm the intricacies of the eight parts of speech, and then sit back and wait for us to ask him a question, anything at all that we didn't understand. Someone would raise a hand and ask something like, "Can you explain the difference between an adjective and an adverb?" and he would leap up and shout back at the foolish student, "You didn't listen! You didn't listen! You've got to learn to pay attention! *Attention! Attention!*"

Only in recent history has the inability to pay attention been given an official diagnostic name: ADD. I think the problem is misnamed; it's not a deficit or lack of attention; the problem is in the *direction* of attention. People are always paying attention, it's just not always being paid to the right source. Sights and sounds from all directions grab our attention. The challenge is to be drawn completely by the one thing we need to be attending to at a given moment. Just like the ocean under the moon, good listeners are seized by the gravitational pull, drawn like waves toward what what is most imporant.

The word *attention* has a word origin that Mr. Martin would love. It comes from the Latin word *attendere*, which literally means *to stretch toward.* I am at an age when I find it necessary to do a series of stretches before engaging in any physical activity. I go just a little beyond my comfort zone and hold the stretch for a sustained period of time. The longer I continue this practice, the longer I find I can stretch. This is a good image for me to think about when I need to engage in active listening. Good listening involves stretching toward the speaker, and more often than not, when I really need to be listening, this stretching will take me out of my comfort zone. Sustaining the stretch — holding it — that is the key. The more you do it, the longer you can stretch.

Sampling Your Life. . .

What does the sacred story and these
random thoughts on *attention* bring to your mind?
What are you stretching toward today?
Sample your own life experience and draw, doodle,
or write what comes to mind.

Catching the Waves of Active Listening

Week Seven: *Filtering*
are you picking up a good signal?

Sampling the Sacred Story

Then David stood at the mouth of the cave and called to Saul,
"My master! My king!" Saul looked back.
David fell to his knees and bowed in reverence.
He called out, "Why do you listen to those who say
'David is out to get you'?"
—Exodus 15:26

The Loop

Why do you listen to those who say. . . ?

Are there some things you wish people
would just stop listening to?
When there are many voices competing for your attention,
how to you filter out those you don't need to listen to?

White Noise
random sampling of *filters*

The ocean wild like an organ played,
the seaweed wove its strands.
The crashin' waves like cymbals clashed
against the rocks and sands.
—Bob Dylan

Kim and I are both lifelong fans of the Atlanta Braves, remembering the days when they were dwelt in the cellar, with Henry Aaron generating the only excitement the team could muster. Because we both grew up listening to the games on the radio, we have a nostalgic preference for radio over television broadcasts. We used to listen to Skip Carey and Don Sutton describe the plays over the radio, leaving room for the imagination to picture the plays, and since we didn't have cable, we got to use our imaginations a lot.

There were only two problems with listening to the Braves on the radio. One, Skip made every routine fly ball sound like a potential home run, and this got annoying after the thousandth time you heard him excitedly shout *it's a long drive* only to find the centerfielder had to take two steps to his right to catch the lazy fly. And two, we didn't have very good reception at our house. We could barely pick up AM 750 on a clear night. On cloudy nights, we'd adjust the dial on the bedside radio ever so slightly, trying to pick up the familiar ballpark sounds, and suddenly out of the white noise it would emerge — Skip making a wise-crack or Don describing the perils of throwing a slider on a 3-2 count with a runner on. And then, just as we got comfortable, the static would creep back in and the signal would disappear. We found that sometimes it worked to pick up the radio and hold it at different angles. That radio gave us some excruciating moments. Imagine the good guys trailing by one with two out in the bottom of the ninth and a runner on second. Skip makes the call: *Chipper digs in to face the left hander. Here's the pitch — it's a deep shot, Van Slyke goes back, back, he's on the warning track he leaps. . .* and then white noise suddenly takes over and you can only guess whether it's a game winner or out three.

An old friend used to say that *it doesn't help to turn the volume up if you're tuned to the wrong station.* In a lot of conversations in our culture today, there's no lack of volume, but lots of people are tuning in to the wrong stations – stations of hate and disrespect. Clear signals of respect are too rare. Good listening requires us to work hard to find a good station, to filter out all the white noise that blocks out reception of clear thinking and common sense and civility. On cloudy nights, it's worth holding our conversations up at every angle possible angle, in hopes that a clear signal will eventually emerge.

Sampling Your Life. . .

What does the sacred story and these random thoughts on *filters* bring to your mind? What kind of noise is cluttering the airwaves for you today? Sample your own life experience and draw, doodle, or write what comes to mind.

Catching the Waves of Active Listening

Week Eight: *Feedback*
are you getting any response?

Sampling the Sacred Story

A third time the LORD called, "Samuel!"
And Samuel got up and went to Eli and said,
"Here I am; you called me." Then Eli realized that
the LORD was calling the boy. So Eli told Samuel,
"Go and lie down, and if he calls you, say,
'Speak, LORD, for your servant is listening.'"
So Samuel went and lay down in his place.
The LORD came and stood there, calling as at the
other times, "Samuel! Samuel!" Then Samuel said,
"Speak, for your servant is listening."

The Loop

Speak, for your servant is listening.

Do you ever wonder if you've heard something right,
and need to check it out to make sure?
Has someone ever said something to you, and
you thought there was more than one message
being sent - one on the surface and one below the surface?
Have you ever thought about the possibility of God
speaking to you through other people, that maybe there's a
hidden message beneath what they are saying to you?

49

I Got The Beat
random sampling of *feedback*

Singing to an ocean, I can hear the ocean's roar.
—Led Zeppelin

My first lesson in piano tuning completely bumfuzzled me. My Uncle Jim taught me that you have to actually get the strings slightly out of tune, to create what he called "the beat." "What beat?" I asked. He struck a key. "*That* beat. Here, I'll speed it up" and he turned the tuning hammer slightly. "Now I'll slow it down," and turned it back. I didn't hear any beat.

Jim tried to explain why the beat was so important. He called it setting the "temper" between the middle 8 notes of the piano. He said that you had to intentionally put the middle octave slightly out of tune, and then tune the rest of the piano to those middle strings, so that there wouldn't be *wolves*. "What are wolves?" I asked. He explained that if you try to tune pianos perfectly, you can get it so that some chords are in perfect harmony, but doing so creates awful howling sounds from other chords, like piercing feedback from a microphone. *Wolves.* Somebody figured out the "tempering" system to spread out the off-key sounds equally across the keyboard, so that while there were no perfect harmonies, neither were there any howling wolves. The "beats" actually create a balance of rich undertones and overtones, those sounds beneath the surface that make piano music so beautiful.

Hard as I tried, I couldn't hear the beat. Jim told me to keep trying, it would happen. I kept tuning and kept tuning, and sure enough, after a few hours, out of nowhere I heard something. A wave, a beat. Wa-wa-wa-wa-wa. It sped up as I turned the hammer, and slowed down as I brought it back toward unison. I couldn't believe it! It was there all the time. I jumped up from the piano bench and ran around the house, shouting out, *I got the beat! I got the beat!*

The beat provides a great image for listening. There's so much to hear under the surface. Think about the people you find it difficult to listen to, conversations that wear you out because you don't like what you hear on the surface. We assume from the outset that these people are out of tune, off key. But if we can think about the beat, the undertones and overtones of their lives, it can change the conversation and add a certain richness to the relationship. I might wonder what beat is created when I add the string of my thought to theirs. Ands when the conversation gets so out of tune that it begins to sound like wolves howling, maybe it's because we have *lost our temper* and need to *temper our relationship* and restore some balance. It's *feedback* that tells us one or both of us is caught up in a quest for perfection — for a beat-less harmony. Letting go of this quest is what makes the undertones and overtones of life possible. Listen – can you hear it? *Wa-wa-wa-wa-wa.* . . . .

Sampling Your Life. . .

What does the sacred story and these
random thoughts on *feedback* bring to your mind?
What are hearing beneath the surface today?
Sample your own life experience and draw, doodle,
or write what comes to mind.

Part Three

Diving into the
Lake of Courage

Diving into the
Lake of Courage

Week Nine: *Risk*
what kind of chances do you take?

Sampling the Sacred Story

Shortly before dawn Jesus went out to them,
walking on the lake. When the disciples saw him
walking on the lake, they were terrified.
"It's a ghost," they said, and cried out in fear.
But Jesus immediately said to them:
"Take courage! It is I. Don't be afraid."

The Loop

Take courage. . . Don't be afraid.

What are some of the risks you think
God is calling you to make?
What does it mean for you to "step out of the boat"
in the midst of a storm of life?

No Lifeguard on Duty
random sampling of *risk*

"God, grant us the courage to risk
something big for something good."
–William Sloane Coffin

When I was in high school I had a part time job at Curious Cargo, a store that sold lots of doodads in the Asheville Mall. Mopping the floor after closing was one of my tasks. In an attempt to make this mundane task tolerable, my co-worker Chris and I created some artwork on the side of the gray metal mop bucket. We painted a picture of the Loch Ness, complete with the monster rising out of the lake, and we attached a sign to the top of the bucket: "No Lifeguard on Duty — Swim at Your Own Risk." By the end of the chore the mop water did look fairly ominous.

The earliest written reference to the Loch Ness monster is found in the biography of Saint Columba, who is credited with bringing Christianity to Scotland. Columba was on his way to visit a Pictish king in 565 C.E. when he stopped along the shore of Loch Ness. He saw a large monster preparing to attack a swimmer. Columba called on God's help, raised his hand, and commanded the beast to "go back with all speed." The monster retreated and the swimmer was saved. Because of this episode and countless other sightings, the sign "swim at your own risk" takes on a whole new meaning in Loch Ness.

"At your own risk." There is a lot of concern now about "at-risk behavior" among youth. Binge drinking, drug use, and unsafe sex are the usual suspects. The term "at-risk children" is used to describe children with particular challenges in life, often due to poverty. Others note, and rightly so, that all children are at risk. While it is common sense to recognize that children suffering the effects of poverty are more vulnerable than children with all available resources at hand, it is also common sense to recognize risk as a reality for all children.

Providing a safe haven for children is one of the key roles, not only for parents, but for everyone in the village that it takes to raise a child. Minimizing unnecessary risks and at-risk behavior is part of the deal. But an obvious dilemma emerges from this quest to risk-proof children. How will they ever learn to take *appropriate* risks? There's little doubt that the teenage years will provide more than enough opportunity for *inappropriate* risk-taking. But where do young people learn to cultivate the courage, the heart, to jump fences and dive into ponds when the situation calls for them to risk something big for something good?

Sampling Your Life. . .

What does the sacred story and these
random thoughts on *risk* bring to your mind? In
what ways are you "at-risk" today?
Sample your own life experience and draw, doodle,
or write what comes to mind.

Diving into the Lake of Courage

Week Ten: *Perseverance*
what keeps you going?

Sampling the Sacred Story

That day when evening came, he said to his disciples, "Let us go over to the other side." Leaving the crowd behind, they took him along, just as he was, in the boat. There were also other boats with him. A furious squall came up, and the waves broke over the boat, so that it was nearly swamped. Jesus was in the stern, sleeping on a cushion. The disciples woke him and said to him, "Teacher, don't you care if we drown?" He got up, rebuked the wind and said to the waves, "Quiet! Be still!" Then the wind died down and it was completely calm. He said to his disciples, "Why are you so afraid? Do you still have no faith?" They were terrified and asked each other, "Who is this? Even the wind and the waves obey him!"

The Loop

Why are you so afraid?
Do you still have no faith?

Do you sometimes feel like giving up and turning back when the going gets rough? What do you think enabled Jesus to sleep peacefully while the storm was raging? How does our faith give us the determination to keep going, to persevere, through tough times?

Keeping On
random sampling of *perseverance*

*Have courage for the great sorrows of life and
patience for the small ones. And when you have
laboriously accomplished your daily task,
go to sleep in peace. God is awake.*
−Victor Hugo

The Salish, a native tribe living in the Pacific northwest, remember ancient stories of a strange marine creature in Lake Okanagan. They call the monster N'ha-a-itk, "Devil of the Lake." These native people, who depended on the lake for survival, carefully surveyed the waters before setting out for fishing expeditions. Later European settlers believe the stories of something large and unusual lurking in these waters with depths close to 1,000 feet. The Salish persevered in the region now known as British Columbia for thousands of years, with a staying power that endured harsh winters, a stark environment, and European conquest. The Devil of the Lake represented deep, persistent fears that had to be faced with stubborn courage and a determined heart.

I learned a lot about stubborn determination during the highlight of my one years as a Boy Scout: going to Camp Daniel Boone for the annual Jamboree with all the regional troops. This was a highly competitive affair. Many of the competitions took place on the lake. There was the free-for-all battle for the greased watermelon, the canoe race, and a relay race where you had to blow a ping-pong ball across the surface of the water. Several of the competitions were endurance tests: who could tread water the longest with their hands in the air, who could swim the farthest, and my activity: who could stand up the longest on the pine log that floated out in the lake. There is no way they would allow children to do this activity these days—it's a broken neck waiting to happen. I think I was more foolish than courageous to volunteer for this event, but I did have good balance and thought I could at least last stay on for the required two minutes to qualify for the semifinal round. My practice rounds left me with bruises all over — I think this might be the source of my back pain now. I found that the secret was to keep moving, keep my feet moving; trying to stand still was a quick way off the log. I am proud to claim, though, that not only did I stand up for the two minutes in the opening round, I made it all the way to the championship round and won the competition by staying on the log for 3 minutes and 15 seconds. At 3 minutes 16 seconds my backside was hitting the log, but the pain was worth the exhilaration of my fellow Troop 22 teammates as they cheered me on.

So what does standing on a log in a lake have to do with courage? As foolish an activity as it was, it showed me the importance of endurance, or perseverance, of getting back up after being thrown down. It taught me what endurance feels like, the rewards that come from sticking with a tough challenge. These were the same kinds of rewards that must have kept the Salish persevering and enduring the monstrous winters around Lake Okanagan. They had the courage to stick with it against impossible odds.

Sampling Your Life. . .

What does the sacred story and these random thoughts on *perseverance* bring to mind? What difficulties are you having to trudge through today? Sample your own life experience and draw, doodle, or write what comes to mind.

Diving into the Lake of Courage

Week Eleven: *Confrontation*
what dangers do you meet head-on?

Sampling the Sacred Story

At once the Spirit sent Jesus out into the wilderness, and he
was in the wilderness forty days,
being tempted by Satan.
He was with the wild animals,
and angels attended him.
−Mark 1:12-13

The Loop

He was with the wild animals.

Why do you think the Holy Spirit drove Jesus into the
wilderness, to confront the devil and the wild animals? Have
you ever had a spiritual "wilderness experience?"
What kinds of things do you think God wants you
to be willing to confront in your life?

Get in the Boat
random sampling of *confrontation*

This is in the end the only kind
of courage that is required of us: the courage
to face the strangest, most unusual,
most inexplicable experiences that can meet us.
—Rainer Maria Rilke, *Letters to a Young Poet*

On the border of what is now Vermont and Canada, a stormy lake was named for Samuel Champlain, the French explorer who founded Quebec. The lake monster residing there, known by the Europeans as "Champ," was known by the native Iroquois tribe as Tataskok. Whatever fear Tataskok represented for the native people prior to the arrival of the explorers, it must have been mild compared to the terrors the Europeans wrought in the war on the "Indians." The Europeans indeed became the "Champs" in their war of terror on the native people of North and South America, in the heartless quest for control of the land.

The confrontation between the colonizers and the native Americans is a tragic demonstration of the inability of two diverse groups, two conflicting ways of life, to co-exist. More precisely, it is the tragedy of the inability of the stronger group to live peaceably alongside people who offer another way of life. This temptation to destroy or conquer the things we don't understand is a tragedy of biblical proportions.

In the Bible another stormy lake, called the Sea of Galilee, divided two historic enemies, Arabs and Jews.

In the gospel of Mark we see Jesus and his disciples taking several boat trips across this lake. Each time the disciples cross over to the east side of the lake, to the unfamiliar land of their enemies, the lake rages in a mighty storm. And then, each time they cross back to their home turf on the west side, it is smooth sailing. But here's the interesting thing: the exact same activities take place on each side of the lake. Jesus feeds the hungry on home turf and behind enemy lines. He heals the sick on both sides. He casts out evil spirits on both sides.

If we are ever going to make headway in work for the common good, we'll sometimes find ourselves on a fearful journey toward strange land, toward people who don't look like us or think like us or act like us. We go back and forth across the lake, with stormy journeys toward the strangers who are different and peaceful journeys back home.

There's nothing new about people entering unfamiliar territory and encountering strangers. The new plot of this story teaches us that we don't have to travel to the strange land in order to destroy or conquer, to become "Champs." Instead, we are likely to discover the same work needing to be done among the strangers as we need among our home folk: feeding the hungry, healing the sick, casting out bad spirits that threaten to destroy community. Traveling into enemy territory and listening for what people are hungry for, seeing where they are wounded, and helping them deal with what drives them crazy, this takes far more courage than the quest to conquer.

Sampling Your Life. . .

What does the sacred story and these
random thoughts on *confrontation* bring to mind?
What are you being called to face head-on today?
Sample your own life experience and draw, doodle,
or write what comes to mind.

Diving into the Lake of Courage

Week Twelve: *Sacrifice*
what's on the line?

Sampling the Sacred Story

*But Jonah ran away from the LORD and headed for
Tarshish. He went down to Joppa, where he found a ship
bound for that port. After paying the fare, he went aboard
and sailed for Tarshish to flee from the LORD. Then the
LORD sent a great wind on the sea, and such a violent
storm arose that the ship threatened to break up. All the
sailors were afraid and each cried out to his own god. And
they threw the cargo into the sea to lighten the ship. . .
The sea was getting rougher and rougher.
So they asked him, "What should we do to you
to make the sea calm down for us?"
"Pick me up and throw me into the sea," he replied, "and it
will become calm. I know that it is my fault
that this great storm has come upon you."*
–Jonah 1:3-5,11-12

The Loop

Pick me up and throw me into the sea.

What do you think gave Jonah the courage to make that
sacrifice? Romans 12 tells us to make our bodies
a "living sacrifice." What do you think that means?
What kinds of things are you willing
to sacrifice for the cause of Christ?

Clash of Titans
random sampling of *sacrifice*

The stories of past courage can define that ingredient — they can teach, they can offer hope, they can provide inspiration. But they cannot supply courage itself. For this everyone must look into their own soul.
       –John F. Kennedy

Sometimes frightening things emerge in the most unexpected places. I don't usually think of Sweden as a scary place, with monsters lurking. I associate Sweden with meatballs and blond volleyball players. But like so many places around the world, Sweden has its own lake monster: Storsjöodjuret. This "Great Lake Monster" reigns terror in Lake Storsjön, in the middle of the peaceful country. You just never know where or when monsters are going to crawl up and bite you.

When I was in college, I led summer activities for my church youth group. One of the annual events was a camping trip out on an island at Lake James. Lake James, like Lake Storsjön in Sweden, is in the middle of a peaceful region where you wouldn't expect monsters to reside. Activities included skiing, fishing, cooking out, and singing songs around the campfire. Nothing to fear — until a few of the guys challenged me to join them for a game of lake football. A monster suddenly rose up out of the deep waters of my memory — the idea of this scared me to death. See, I had broken my arm in two places playing football a few years earlier, and the excruciating pain of that experience led me to vow never to pick up a football again. To make matters worse, the youth group included several players from the local high school conference championship football team. I would never have been crazy enough to step on a field with these guys, who were twice my size. But for some foolish reason I agreed to confront the monster and play the lake version, figuring that the weightlessness of the water would even things out. The games turned out to be a bona fide clash of the titans. The guys played with great gusto, creaming each other and dunking each other and often yelling out their favorite phrase: "Sacrifice the body!" Thankfully, these "sacrifices" didn't involve any more broken bones, and I survived the games with only bruises to show for my efforts.

Sacrifice. The word literally means "to make holy." It takes heart — courage — to know when and where to make a real sacrifice (the root word for *courage* is an old Latin word, *cor*, meaning *heart)*. The real heart-wrenching decisions in life come when you have to choose between two good things—when you have to sacrifice something good, something valuable, in order to get or keep something better. These are the real titanic clashes — when you have to give up something precious in order to have something more precious. That's what makes life holy.

Sampling Your Life. . .

What does the sacred story and these
random thoughts on *sacrifice* bring to your mind?
What good thing do you need to let go of today
in order to choose the best thing?
Sample your own life experience and draw, doodle,
or write what comes to mind.

Made in the USA
Charleston, SC
28 September 2011